Effective Mediation
Techniques for Resolving Even the Toughest Conflicts

Jean Ruth Harris

Table of Contents

1. Introduction 2
2. Understanding Conflict: Causes and Consequences 3
   - 2.1. Unraveling Conflict 3
   - 2.2. Causes of Conflict 3
   - 2.3. Consequences of Conflict 4
3. The Power within Mediation: An Introduction 7
   - 3.1. Unveiling the Concept of Mediation 7
   - 3.2. The Power Spectrum of Mediation: From Personal to Global . 8
   - 3.3. Techniques and Approaches within Mediation 8
   - 3.4. Mediation in the Modern Era: An Indispensable Tool for Peace 9
4. Psychology of Conflict Resolution: A Deep-Dive 10
   - 4.1. Emotions and Conflict 10
   - 4.2. Understanding the Role of Perception 11
   - 4.3. The Impact of Communication 11
   - 4.4. The Use of Cognitive Behavioral Techniques 12
   - 4.5. Mindfulness: The Art of Being Present 12
5. Communicative Techniques for Mediators 14
   - 5.1. Deconstructing The Iceberg: Elements of Communication ... 14
   - 5.2. The Art of Active Listening 15
   - 5.3. Emotional Intelligence in Communication 15
   - 5.4. The Power of Questions 15
   - 5.5. Encouraging Participation through Inclusive Communication 16
   - 5.6. Assertive Communication: Balancing Respect and Directness 16
   - 5.7. Feedback: A Tool for Confirmation and Corrections 16
   - 5.8. Navigating Difficult Conversations 17

6. Diffusing Tension: The Role of Emotional Intelligence 18
   6.1. The Birth of Emotional Intelligence 18
   6.2. Understanding Emotions: The Heartbeat of Emotional Intelligence 19
   6.3. The Application of Emotional Intelligence in Mediation 19
   6.4. Emotional Self-Management: The Anchor of Emotional Stability 20
   6.5. Emotional Intelligence: A Tool for Empathy 20
   6.6. Emotional Intelligence: Active Listening 21
   6.7. Emotional Intelligence: The Silver Lining in Diffusing Tension 21

7. Strategies for Encouraging Cooperation and Collaboration 23
   7.1. The Role of Trust and Transparency 23
   7.2. The Power of Active Listening 24
   7.3. Encouraging Engagement and Participation 24
   7.4. Building Relationships through Empathy 24
   7.5. Employing Problem-solving techniques 25
   7.6. Conclusion: The Mediator as a Facilitator 25

8. Case Studies: Mediation Success Stories 27
   8.1. The Cuban Missile Crisis 27
   8.2. The Aceh Peace Agreement 28
   8.3. The Good Friday Agreement 28

9. Overcoming Challenges in Mediation 30
   9.1. Understanding Challenges in Mediation 30
   9.2. Managing Emotions in Mediation 30
   9.3. Bridging Cultural and Linguistic Differences 31
   9.4. Dealing with Power Imbalances 31
   9.5. Overcoming Resistance to Solution 32
   9.6. Conclusion 32

10. Advanced Mediation Techniques: From Theory to Practice 34

- 10.1. Advanced Mediation Techniques: The Toolbox 34
- 10.2. Case in Point: Putting Techniques into Practice 35
- 10.3. Mastering Advanced Mediation Techniques: Inner Growth . 36
- 11. Sustaining Peace: The Aftermath of Mediation 38
  - 11.1. Aftermath Observations 38
  - 11.2. Fortifying the Outcomes 39
  - 11.3. Preventing Recurrences 39

Peace is not absence of conflict, it is the ability to handle conflict by peaceful means.

— Ronald Reagan

Chapter 1. Introduction

In an increasingly polarized world, effective conflict resolution has ascended the ranks of pivotal skills one can acquire. Our Special Report titled "Effective Mediation: Techniques for Resolving Even the Toughest Conflicts" is a captivating deep dive into the art and science of pacifying disputes. Sit back, let your imagination unfurl its wings as it navigates through persuasive negotiation strategies, immersive case studies, and invaluable insights from seasoned peace facilitators. Whether you're a classroom teacher, top-level executive, or curious lifelong learner, this report promises a transformative journey, armoring you with techniques to dissolve the highest stake disputes with elegance and grace. Let this be the beacon leading you to the shore of peace and effective conflict resolution. You won't just read about conflict resolution – you'll breathe it, live it, embody it. What better time than now to invest in harmony? Don't just dream of a conflict-free world – become its architect with our Special Report!

Chapter 2. Understanding Conflict: Causes and Consequences

Conflict, a discord of action, feeling, or effect, is a multifaceted subject of interest for psychologists, sociologists, anthropologists, and conflict resolution practitioners. It is encountered in every strata of our society—from interpersonal relationships to corporate settings and even between nations. Before delving into the causes and consequences of conflict, let's reassess our understanding of what encompasses 'conflict'.

2.1. Unraveling Conflict

A misunderstanding shrouded with emotions doesn't always qualify as conflict. A rich tapestry woven by differences of opinion, a tussle of interests, or a battle of personal values, conflict is a complexity that goes beyond mere disputes. It finds roots in variances, whether they're cultural, philosophical, financial, or political. This doesn't paint conflict as necessarily negative; conflict, when navigated skilfully, can catalyze growth, innovation, and stronger interpersonal relations.

2.2. Causes of Conflict

To get to the crux of conflict resolution, understanding the core causes of conflict is an indispensable undertaking.

1. Competing Interests: When individuals or groups have disparate goals which cannot be achieved simultaneously, conflict arises. The struggle for resources, positional authority, or undue advantage are prime examples.

2. Communication Breakdown: Misunderstandings and misinterpretations bred by ineffective or insufficient communication often lay the groundwork for persistent conflict. Cultural differences and language barriers exacerbate this issue.

3. Power Dynamics: Hierarchical disparities or attempts for dominance often sow seeds of conflict. This could be in the form of overt authority or subtler forms of power play that build tension.

4. Personality Clashes: Empirical evidence corroborates that incompatibility between individuals, whether that's in work style or personal values, can initiate conflict.

Recognizing the causes is the first step towards propelling oneself onto the platform for effective conflict resolution. But herein lies a significant question: why bother resolving conflict? What implications does unmitigated conflict carry? Should we be concerned?

2.3. Consequences of Conflict

The ripple effects of conflict aren't confined to its immediate locus, but oscillate to cause widespread repercussions. Here's a look at the major consequences:

1. Damage to Relationships: Ongoing conflict creates a chasm between individuals and groups, eroding trust, empathy and often leading to active avoidance. It hinders collaboration and, at its worst, can cause irreparable damage to personal and professional relationships.

2. Reduced Productivity: In a professional context, conflict saps the energy of team members, diverting their focus from achieving common goals towards either diffusing tensions or engaging in them. This results in a significant drop in productivity.

3. Tarnished Reputation: Unresolved conflict can affect bystanders

or external parties involved, leading to reputational damage. Especially for businesses, it could perturb customer loyalty and negatively impact profitability.

4. Impact on Health: Research has linked prolonged conflict to an array of health issues, ranging from sleep disorders to mental health conditions like anxiety, depression, and even increased risk of cardiovascular diseases.

However, not all consequences of conflict are negative. As paradoxical as it might seem, conflict presents an opportunity for growth and development.

1. Instigates Change: The non-conformist nature of conflict challenges the status quo, paving the way for innovation and creative problem solving.
2. Self-Awareness: Conflict forces individuals to introspect, understand their priorities and reevaluate their approach, fostering self-awareness and personal improvement.
3. Strengthens Connections: When conflicts are resolved healthily, they can give rise to a stronger bond between the parties involved—be it personal or professional—a relationship fortified by understanding and empathy.

Understanding conflict—causes and its consequences—forms the cornerstone of effective conflict management. The ability to comprehend and decipher conflict roots sets the stage for effective dialogue, negotiation, and problem-solving strategies, all of which are crucial in the highly acclaimed field of mediation.

This chapter attempts to encapsulate a comprehensive understanding of conflict, utilizing numerous scholarly resources, theories, and empirical studies to illustrate its causes and consequences. With an evolving understanding of this phenomenon, we move a step closer to the ultimate goal: the attainment of conflict resolution, thereby enabling a more harmonious coexistence in this increasingly polarized world.

Chapter 3. The Power within Mediation: An Introduction

In order to grasp the complexity and application of mediation and its integral role in conflict resolution, it's vital to start by laying the groundwork for understanding its inherent power. Mediation exists as an aegis, the array of skills and strategies it encompasses serves to shield individuals involved in a conflict from further harm, disruption, or misunderstanding. It encourages dialogue, fosters understanding, and enkindles paths towards resolution that may have otherwise remained obscured by contesting disputes.

3.1. Unveiling the Concept of Mediation

Mediation, at its core, is a process where a neutral third party, aptly denominated as a 'mediator', assists two or more figures embroiled in a conflict in reaching an agreement. The critical aspect to remember here is that the mediator does not impose a solution. Instead, they facilitate a platform where individuals can freely express their perspectives, needs, and desires. The mediator's role is to guide these individuals towards mutually beneficial outcomes by promoting communication, empathy, and cooperation.

The power within mediation lies fundamentally within its emphasis on 'self-determination' and 'empowerment'. Parties to the conflict remain the decision-makers, retaining the autonomy to agree or not agree to terms – a characteristic distinguishing mediation from other forms of resolution like arbitration or litigation, where the final decision descends from an external authority. This foundational principle magnifies the intrinsic value of mediation, exchanging a fight for control with an embrace of understanding.

3.2. The Power Spectrum of Mediation: From Personal to Global

Comprehending the power within mediation involves a trek across different terrain - from personal conflicts to intricate international disputes. At base, mediation extends beyond arbitrating quotidian discord, stretching into realms such as family disputes, commercial disagreements, workplace unrest, communal clashes, and even international tensions. Each arena implies unique challenges yet also unveils the malleable nature of mediation - an effective tool adaptable for varied conflict characteristics.

Understanding this spectrum offers considerable insight into the functions and significance of mediation. For instance, in the realm of family disputes, the power of mediation manifests when it helps families navigate emotionally charged disagreements. Similarly, its power is illustrated when resolving international disputes, where intricate negotiations can affect national relationships and global peace.

3.3. Techniques and Approaches within Mediation

Broadly, the techniques and approaches adopted within the mediation process are aimed towards providing a safe space for discussion, minimizing hostility, identifying common ground, and creating an environment conducive to cooperation. Some of these methods include:

- Active listening: Allows participants to feel understood and appreciated.
- Reframing: Encourages more positive communication by reconstructing negatively charged statements into neutral or

positive ones.

- Identifying interests: Penetrates surface contentions to expose underlying needs and desires.
- Generating options: Encourages creativity to conceive a variety of resolution approaches.
- Reality testing: Probes to verify the feasibility of proposed solutions.

Such techniques empower mediators to transform a space of conflict into a space of negotiation, enabling parties to communicate, connect, and collaborate more effectively.

3.4. Mediation in the Modern Era: An Indispensable Tool for Peace

In our modern societal configuration, riddled with complexity and divergence of interests, mediation adopts an ever more pressing relevance. As crucial decisions, actions, and reactions teeter on the precipice between collaboration and conflict, mediators emerge as essential peacekeepers, striving to bridge gaps and mend fractures with the power of dialogue and understanding.

In the contemporary global landscape, mediators stand as guardians at the crossroads of decision-making, helping navigate through intricate interplays of power, interests, and justice. Equipped with the nuanced understanding of its applications and the resulting societal impact, one can truly comprehend the realm of mediation - a potent tool for fostering relationships, resolving conflicts, and sculpting a more peaceful world. This is the power within mediation – a power that lies in every conversation, every understanding, and every choice that leads us towards resolution and peace.

Chapter 4. Psychology of Conflict Resolution: A Deep-Dive

Homo sapiens, or 'wise man' in Latin, our species is blessed, or perhaps burdened, with the capacities for reflection, anticipation, and manipulation. These intellectual capabilities, when coupled with the intricate and complex nature of human relationships, often breed contention—a psychological tug-of-war fueling conflict. In this chapter, we aim to delve into the powerhouse that is the human mind and unearth some rational underpinnings of conflict while exploring promising psychological strategies for its resolution.

4.1. Emotions and Conflict

Emotions blaze the trail of human interaction. They are an essential aspect of our daily life and determine how we react to the world around us. They mold our responses, influence our perceptions, and to a large extent, dictate our behaviors. We see a reflection of this in conflict. Different emotions like anger, frustration, fear serve as both precursors and consequences of a disagreement, in turn amplifying the conflict itself. Understanding how emotions cater to conflict is therefore paramount.

When evaluating conflict through the lens of emotions, two significant points warrant attention. First, conflicts are associated with negative emotions such as resentment and hostility, which reduce our capacity to communicate, cooperate, and understand the perspectives of others. Our thinking becomes rigid, resistant to new possibilities and alternative viewpoints. Second, these emotions can prompt reactive and retaliatory behavior, which can heighten the severity of the conflict. Our emotional state, thus, sets the stage for the escalation or de-escalation of a disagreement. We must learn to recognize and manage our emotional state effectively to prevent further compounding of conflict.

4.2. Understanding the Role of Perception

Perception is an imperative influencer in conflict resolution. It determines how we understand and interpret the sentiments of others. When perception is clouded by negative bias or erroneous assumptions, it sparks conflict and impedes resolution. A lens colored by false impressions and prejudices enlarges differences and minimizes similarities.

It's crucial to remember that perception is inherently subjective. Even when presented with identical situations, individuals can interpret them differently based on their personal experiences, beliefs, values, and the social or cultural milieu from which they hail. Thus, an individual's perception of a conflict can greatly differ from that of others involved in the dispute. Embracing this subjectivity can significantly bolster our conflict resolution efforts.

4.3. The Impact of Communication

Communication is the bridge between isolation and understanding. It matters not just what we communicate, but how we do so. Herein, understanding the concept of "confirmation bias" is critical. This phenomenon describes our propensity to interpret, favor, and remember information that confirms our pre-existing beliefs or values. It is a formidable barrier to conflict resolution as it fuels misunderstandings and fortifies resistance to alternate viewpoints.

To circumvent confirmation bias, active listening, non-defensive communication, empathy, and assertiveness, strides towards open and truthful communication, which is the pathway to a breakthrough in conflicts.

4.4. The Use of Cognitive Behavioral Techniques

Cognitive Behavioral Techniques (CBTs) facilitate greater self-awareness, challenge distorted cognitions, and promote healthier patterns of thinking. Their application in conflict resolution derives from the understanding that our thoughts, feelings, and behaviors are intricately intertwined.

CBTs serve to challenge and rectify cognitive distortions that can breed conflict. These distortions, including 'all-or-nothing' thinking, catastrophizing, mind reading, and overgeneralization, impede a balanced and rational approach to conflict resolution. By helping individuals recognize and challenge these cognitive distortions, CBTs pave the way for healthier and less contentious interpersonal relationships.

4.5. Mindfulness: The Art of Being Present

Another valuable approach to conflict resolution resides in the practice of mindfulness. Mindfulness is the psychological process of purposefully bringing one's attention to experiences occurring in the present moment without judgment. Mindfulness can aid conflict resolution by promoting empathy, reducing stress, cultivating emotional intelligence, and fostering a stronger sense of shared reality.

In the throes of conflict, taking a mindful approach determines our ability to step back, analyze the situation objectively and respond thoughtfully. It aids us in more genuine connections with others, fostering improved interpersonal dynamics and communication.

In conclusion, the human psyche, an intricate web of perceptions, emotions, cognitions, is where conflict both begins and can potentially end. Approached with empathy and understanding, psychology presents a promising avenue into resolving conflicts in a harmonious manner, opening doors to cooperation, cohesion and peace.

Chapter 5. Communicative Techniques for Mediators

Effective communication forms the cornerstone of successful mediation. The finest negotiators and peacemakers fully understand the importance of not just talking, but talking effectively. Various techniques and strategies act as arrows in their quiver, allowing them to navigate across a tumultuous sea of disputes and bring the ship safely to the shore of mutual agreement. The communicator serves as the catalyst, cutting through the cacophony, and helping to create harmony where discord once reigned.

5.1. Deconstructing The Iceberg: Elements of Communication

Communication, like an iceberg, has much more beneath the surface than one sees at first glance. It involves three dimensions: verbal, non-verbal, and paraverbal, each having its part in the grand choreography of human interaction.

Verbal Communication: Involves spoken words and their semantic interpretation. Crucial in relaying factual information and explicit messages. When used effectively, it can clarify misunderstandings, and convey sincere understanding, acknowledgment, or even apologies.

Non-verbal Communication: Actions often speak louder than words. This sub-dimension includes facial expressions, body movements, gestures, and postures. These signals play a crucial role in conveying empathy, building rapport and trust.

Paraverbal Communication: The 'how' in communication. It deals with the tonal, pitch, pace, volume, and voice modulation aspects. It lends emotion and intent to the spoken words, making or breaking relationships, setting the tone of interactions.

5.2. The Art of Active Listening

Among the medley of communicative techniques, active listening stands as a pillar of strength. It demands full attention, genuine curiosity, and non-judgmental openness to the speaker's viewpoint. Nodding in acknowledgment, infusing pauses for comprehension, paraphrasing for understanding, summarization, and probing with relevant questions, all form integral parts of active listening. This practice cultivates a safe environment that encourages open dialogue, making participants feel heard and validated, often leading to more productive discussion and eventual resolution.

5.3. Emotional Intelligence in Communication

Emotional intelligence escalates communicative efficiency manifold. It allows mediators to grasp the emotional undercurrents of disputes, discern implicit messages, and respond with sensitivity. Understanding and regulating one's emotions, empathizing with others, and using emotions to facilitate thinking are paramount skills in empathetic, effective communication. Emotional intelligence is a mediator's key to steering the debate away from personal attacks and towards problem-solving.

5.4. The Power of Questions

Questions, when used mindfully, can unveil layers of information, feelings, and perspectives. Open-ended questions encourage dialogue and foster understanding, serving a dual purpose of gathering information and conveying interest. Contrastingly, closed-ended questions can provide specificity but must be used sparingly to avoid interrogation-like situations. Neutral language, removing accusatory tone or leading phrases, ensures a conducive environment preserved for productive resolution.

5.5. Encouraging Participation through Inclusive Communication

Inclusive language embraces all views, fostering trust and engagement. It includes avoiding discriminatory or offensive words, using gender-neutral terms, being sensitive to cultural nuances, and treating all participants with equal dignity. The mediator's role is to sculpt a conversation that actively reduces the intimidation of the disputants and encourages them to participate and express freely.

5.6. Assertive Communication: Balancing Respect and Directness

Mediators should aim for assertiveness in their communication, harmonizing the twin needs of being respectful yet direct. It involves expressing oneself honestly and openly, while ensuring it does not encroach upon the rights of others. Such a component strikes a balance between passive and aggressive tendencies, minimizing the possibility of misunderstandings or escalated conflicts.

5.7. Feedback: A Tool for Confirmation and Corrections

Effective feedback is an integral part of communication, serving to confirm understandings or to rectify misinterpretations. Feedback should be timely, relevant, specific yet balanced, and constructive. It should aim to clarify, reconcile, and move the conversation towards resolution, and away from personal conflicts.

5.8. Navigating Difficult Conversations

Difficult conversations can often become derailing points in a mediation process. However, when navigated effectively, these become critical junctions for breakthroughs in understanding and resolving conflicts. Staying calm, using 'I' statements to express feelings, focusing on the issue and not the person, seeking common ground, and offering alternatives are major strategies to manage difficult conversations.

In the macrocosm of mediation, communication reigns supreme. Mastery over effective communicative techniques equips mediators with a potent tool, allowing them to tear through the veils of conflict and misunderstanding to achieve resolution. The above techniques serve merely as the starting point of a lifelong journey of continuous learning, adjustment, and refinement in the art of effective communication. Embrace them, embody them and watch as you evolve into a true exemplar of peace facilitation.

Chapter 6. Diffusing Tension: The Role of Emotional Intelligence

The transformative potential held within the captivating realm of Emotional Intelligence (EI) begins with an inquisitive dive into the depths of human emotionality, psychology, and their immeasurable influence on conflict resolution. Navigating this labyrinth is a precursor to the effective diffusion of tensions, the foundation of amicable settlements, and the triumph of peace over conflict.

6.1. The Birth of Emotional Intelligence

In the revelatory realms of psychology and sociology, the birth of emotional intelligence has sparked a renewed interest and diverse dialogues about its efficacy in the broad canvas of human interaction and conflict mediation. When psychologists Peter Salovey and John D. Mayer first introduced this concept in the 1990s, they defined it as a set of skills hypothesized to contribute to the accurate appraisal and expression of emotion in oneself and in others. Appreciating its potential allows us to dissect the intricate narratives woven by our emotional states and responses - understanding, perceiving, using, and managing emotions effectively. Here, these core elements synthesize a powerful, enlightening lens through which worldviews and empathetic understanding flourish, providing the fertile ground where seeds of effective conflict resolution can sprout.

6.2. Understanding Emotions: The Heartbeat of Emotional Intelligence

A comprehensive understanding of emotional intelligence invariably navigates towards the enigmatic reservoir of our emotions - the wellspring of our reactive patterns and relational interactions. Emotions, as raw and unfiltered reflections of our inner state, are the footprints of our conscious and subconscious mind, shaping our perceptions, interpretations, and reactions towards situations, people, and the context around us. Estèphe-Tabouille – a seasoned psychologist and conflict mediator – underscores the importance of emotional literacy, affirming that the ability to recognize, categorize, and articulate our emotional states forms the first rung in the ladder of emotional intelligence, thus becoming a valuable ally in conflict resolution contexts.

6.3. The Application of Emotional Intelligence in Mediation

Invoking the power of emotional intelligence in conflict resolution pivots on identifying, understanding, and effectively managing our emotions and those of others. This can be, and often is, the make-or-break moment in mediation. The application of emotional intelligence comes to life within the crucible of mediation in myriad forms; understanding the emotions at play, managing one's emotional responses, cultivating empathy, and engaging active listening, to name a few.

Navigating Eloise Cucola's crucial 2005 study of the effectiveness of emotional intelligence in divorce mediation, we encounter some invaluable insights. Cucola's research highlighted the correlation between high emotional intelligence and successful mediation outcomes. This pioneering work underscores the importance of a mediator's emotional intelligence when facilitating negotiations, primarily their empathetic abilities, emotion regulation, and use of emotions to foster a constructive dialogue.

6.4. Emotional Self-Management: The Anchor of Emotional Stability

Being in the eye of the storm and managing to stay composed and empathetic is no small feat. However, emotional self-management – an essential facet of EI – equips us with strategies to regulate our emotional responses effectively, ensuring our reactions align with our insights and goals. Feelings of anger, fear, or frustration can easily derail a negotiation. Mastering emotional regulation can help mediators maintain an optimistic, empathetic approach, even in the face of hostile reactions or high-stress situations.

By fostering a self-aware practice of 'response' rather than 'reaction,' we align ourselves with Mediator Sheila Heen's suggestion that "every difficult conversation is essentially about feelings." Here, recognizing and validating the roiling emotions beneath the surface can empower individuals, fostering a sense of shared understanding and mutual respect.

6.5. Emotional Intelligence: A Tool for Empathy

Perhaps one of the most potent aspects of emotional intelligence is its capacity to nurture empathy – the ability to understand and share the feelings of another. This deliberate cultivation of understanding can transform conflict dynamics, enabling the mediator to build a bridge between opposing parties through shared emotional states.

Empathy employs the power of validation, recognizing and acknowledging emotions, and presupposing no judgment. It enables individuals to feel heard and understood. Such recognition often leads to defensiveness subsiding, paving the way for a resolution-centric dialogue.

6.6. Emotional Intelligence: Active Listening

Another significant tool in the emotional intelligence toolkit is active listening – the practice of deeply understanding and reflecting another's perspective – which helps to establish trust and rapport in a conflicting situation. Active listening requires a full focus on the speaker, noting their words, body language, and underlying emotions. It involves providing feedback through verbal and non-verbal cues to demonstrate understanding and attention. This can profoundly enhance the communicative atmosphere, fostering a more open, honest, and resolution-centric dialogue.

6.7. Emotional Intelligence: The Silver Lining in Diffusing Tension

Having explored the vast landscape of emotional intelligence, its role in diffusing tension becomes undeniable. By decoding their emotional states and managing their emotional responses, the parties involved can detoxify a heated situation, temper escalating tensions, and foster an environment more conducive to resolution.

Emotional intelligence, via empathy and active listening, can also aid in dissolving defensive positionings, misunderstandings, and deep-seated fears. Conclusively, emotional intelligence is the beacon that illuminates the path to effective conflict resolution, acting as an invaluable catalyst in the sophisticated dance of mediation.

The result: a leap from vicious cycles of conflict to virtuous cycles of resolution, a transformation made possible, significantly through the power of emotional intelligence. It's no mere theory but a skilled practice, an art in itself, spiraling upwards in a crescendo of empathy, understanding, validation, active listening, and effective communication – all essentials in transforming heated tension into harmonious resolution.

Chapter 7. Strategies for Encouraging Cooperation and Collaboration

Creating an atmosphere permeated with cooperation and collaboration is crucial in mediation. This chapter entails a comprehensive discussion about the strategies mediators can employ to foster an environment of mutual respect and collaboration. Throughout this section, we'll explore methods that underscore the importance of a cooperative process, enhance the chances for a successful resolution, and minimize the aftermath of discord.

7.1. The Role of Trust and Transparency

Trust forms the bedrock of any fruitful interaction. As a mediator, your primary task is to develop and maintain trust between yourself and the parties involved, and importantly, among the parties themselves. This involves transparent communication. Convey every step, every process, every consequence in clear, unambiguous terms. Maintain integrity by ensuring your actions align with your words. Mirroring trust and honesty in your actions establishes a pattern that others would likely follow.

A mediator needs to be neutral, maintaining an unbiased perspective. This impartiality helps foster trust and invites open dialogue. When each party feels they've been heard and understood, they are more likely to cooperate and collaborate.

7.2. The Power of Active Listening

Developing active listening skills is invaluable for a mediator. It involves concentrating, understanding, responding, and remembering what is being said. Active listening transcends hearing the spoken words; It includes comprehending non-verbal cues such as body language and tone of voice.

When mediators demonstrate genuine interest and understanding, parties feel respected and valued. It creates an atmosphere conducive to expressing views openly and honestly, leading to meaningful discussion that aids resolution efforts.

7.3. Encouraging Engagement and Participation

Active involvement from all parties forms the essence of collaborative problem solving. A mediator should strive to ensure everyone has a voice in the process. This is achievable by creating an inclusive environment that values each perspective. Similarly, encouraging questions and dialogue nurtures collective decision making.

It is equally vital to manage power imbalances, as they may hinder participation. Mediators can adopt strategies such as caucus sessions where each party is given private time to discuss concerns. These sessions can recalibrate the power dynamics and ensure more equitable interaction.

7.4. Building Relationships through Empathy

Empathy is the ability to understand and share the feelings of others, stepping into their shoes. It is a powerful tool in mediation that aids in the cultivation of healthy relationships. By showing empathy, a mediator encourages parties to express themselves openly.

Through empathetic communication, a mediator fosters a sense of mutual understanding among the parties. It helps parties perceive their adversary's perspective, breaking down barriers of misunderstanding, and setting the stage for collaboration.

7.5. Employing Problem-solving techniques

Employing problem-solving techniques like brainstorming sessions or mind mapping can encourage cooperation among parties. These techniques stimulate open-mindedness and creativity, empowering parties to arrive at solutions collaboratively. By creating a sense of unity in finding solutions, a sense of teamwork is fostered, easing the resolution process.

7.6. Conclusion: The Mediator as a Facilitator

In essence, a mediator is a facilitator – someone who leads others through a process to a collective decision. Your role is integral in creating an atmosphere conducive to cooperation and collaboration. By promoting trust, ensuring participation, utilizing active listening, demonstrating empathy, and employing problem-solving techniques, mediators stand a higher chance of transforming disputes into mutual agreements.

For, in the end, it is not about 'winning.' Mediation is about finding the common ground, where each party feels respected, heard, and satisfied. It is about forging relationships that have looked beyond conflict and found a pathway to peace. The mediator is the guiding light on this journey.

Endeavor to use these strategies consciously and consistently. You'll likely find that these seemingly small efforts play a tremendous role in shaping effective, successful mediation spaces. Be patient and persistent for the dividends these techniques pay might not be immediate, but in the long run, certainly worthwhile. Yielding the power of cooperation and collaboration is a skill worth developing, for it harbors the potential to convert a battleground into a field of shared understanding and peace.

Chapter 8. Case Studies: Mediation Success Stories

Exploring the field of mediation from an experience-based approach will empower our perspective towards conflict resolution, allowing us to comprehend inherent complexities and solutions closely. Case studies encapsulate historical move-based strategies, and their evaluation often serves as a treasure trove of nuggets to future mediators.

8.1. The Cuban Missile Crisis

Possibly one of the most significant successes in mediation history occurred during the Cuban Missile Crisis. The world beheld a glimpse of nuclear warfare, as the United States and Soviet Union edged dangerously close to a catastrophic conflict. But through the sheer artistry of diplomacy and mediation, they backed down.

These nations found themselves locked into a fierce geo-political contest over the presence of Soviet nuclear missiles in Cuba, a mere 90 miles from United States soil. The crisis peaked when the U.S. discovered construction on the missile sites. In reaction, President John F. Kennedy straightaway imposed a naval blockade — or 'quarantine', as they preferred — around Cuba.

Mediation under such turbulent circumstances needed extraordinary talent, calling for the calmest demeanor and the sharpest negotiation skills. The crucial factor in the resolution was the back-channel communication that was set up between the Kennedy administration and the Kremlin. The third-party role played by U.N. Secretary-General, U Thant, was also pivotal. His proposal of a cooling-off period was welcomed by both sides.

This case study is a testament to strategic communication and the power of mediation, which averted a nuclear disaster and effectively managed one of the most significant conflicts in modern history.

8.2. The Aceh Peace Agreement

Also known as the Helsinki Agreement, the Aceh peace deal is a story that demonstrates how effective communication and mediation can be in achieving peace even in the most challenging circumstances.

In the wake of decades-long violent clash between the Indonesian government and the Free Aceh Movement, the situation was at a standstill. Aceh was seeking independence, whereas the government was aiming for a unified country. The involvement of Martti Ahtisaari, a former Finnish president known for his peacekeeping efforts, shifted the trajectory of the conflict significantly.

Ahtisaari's ability to build a sense of trust with both parties, combined with his comprehensive approach towards issues, was commendable. From economic arrangements to governance, he addressed all aspect diligently. His ultimate role as a mediator led to the signing of the peace deal in 2005, granting Aceh a significant amount of autonomy. Post the agreement, Aceh has shown tremendous progress, experiencing an upswing in socio-economic prosperity.

The study of this mediation process emphasizes the role of trust in mediation and shines a light on the holistic approach often required.

8.3. The Good Friday Agreement

Labelled as one of the most successful peace processes, Northern Ireland's Good Friday Agreement stands as a shining testament to mediation's power. After experiencing violent conflict known as 'The Troubles' for approximately 30 years, Northern Ireland saw the dawn of peace and potential resolution.

Senator George J. Mitchell, delegated as chair of the peace negotiations, employed a mediator's patience and perseverance, fostering a negotiating environment, encouraging parties to come up with solutions. His neutral attitude was crucial in building trust among participants, navigating them through discussions and disagreement to ultimate consensus.

On Good Friday, April 10, 1998, this agreement was signed between the UK and Irish governments and political parties in Northern Ireland. The successful resolution encompassed complex issues like political status, civil and cultural rights, arms decommissioning, and justice. It set up a power-sharing assembly, facilitated prisoner release, and operationalized an equality agenda.

The case illuminates the crucial element of patience and the ability to strive for the middle ground, irrespective of contentious issues at hand.

Each of these case studies poses as a real-world classroom providing a famous spectrum of insights and lessons. They reveal how mediation can combat even the most critical and complex conflicts. It all boils down to the artful play of communication, negotiations, trust-building, patience, and acceptance that paves the way to resolution and peace. It's these very attributes that future peacemakers will need to cultivate and harness if they wish to excel in the landscape of conflict resolution.

Chapter 9. Overcoming Challenges in Mediation

In the dynamic and sometimes convoluted world of mediation, it is inevitable that challenges will arise. These challenges may form due to entrenched positions, emotional outbursts, cultural misunderstandings, and the like. However, with focused intent, a clear strategy, and applied techniques, these hurdles can be effectively overcome.

9.1. Understanding Challenges in Mediation

Mediation is, in essence, a negotiation process. The primary aim is to bring about a resolution that satisfies all parties involved. Overcoming challenges in mediation, thus, begins with an understanding of the problems capable of hindering that goal. In mediation, challenges may manifest in various forms, such as emotional tensions, cultural or language barriers, hostile attitudes, and power imbalances.

Although seasoned mediators usually anticipate such issues, they can sometimes appear unexpectedly and disrupt the mediation process significantly, particularly if they are not addressed promptly and properly. It is crucial, therefore, not just to expect the unexpected, but to remain resilient in the face of such hurdles.

9.2. Managing Emotions in Mediation

Mediation almost always involves disputes that are deeply emotional to the parties concerned. Intense emotions on either side can undermine the resolution efforts, cause breakdowns in communication and strain relationships even further.

To combat this, mediators should employ a variety of emotion regulation techniques. These may include active listening (where the mediator nonjudgmentally reflects back the speaker's feelings), deescalating and reframing emotional language, and allowing space for negative emotions to be expressed and validated without necessarily furthering conflict.

9.3. Bridging Cultural and Linguistic Differences

Mediation can take place between people of diverse backgrounds, each of whom brings their individual cultural values and perspectives to the negotiating table. This diversity, if not carefully navigated, can lead to misinterpretations and mistrust, and even intensify the conflict.

Similarly, language barriers can significantly hamper the mediation process. In such cases, mediators must be prepared to use clear, simple, universally understood language, use translators if necessary, and adopt a flexible, culturally-sensitive approach to mediating issues.

9.4. Dealing with Power Imbalances

Power imbalances, whether based on economic status, gender, race, ability, or other sociocultural factors, can hinder a fair mediation process. Mediators must be vigilant, recognize these imbalances, and take necessary steps to level the playing field, ensuring each party feels heard and that their interests are being fairly represented.

This could mean advocating for more equal speaking time, challenging dominant narratives, or implementing measures to boost the confidence and negotiation power of the lesser powerful party.

9.5. Overcoming Resistance to Solution

It's not uncommon to encounter parties who, due to fixed minds and hardened hearts stemming from past betrayals and mistrust, struggle to align with the resolution process. They may appear stuck or perpetually loop around damaging patterns of communication.

In these situations, mediators can elicit shift by employing various strategies. Rooting out cooperation by focusing on areas of mutual interest, breaking down large issues into smaller, more manageably solved problems, shifting perspectives by reframing the issue, or narrative-mediation, where mediators help parties build a new shared narrative, can all encourage this requisite flexibility.

9.6. Conclusion

By understanding the nature and root of the challenges, employing active listening and deescalation techniques, managing cultural and linguistic differences, addressing power imbalances, and finding ways to unstuck rigid perspectives, mediators can keep the mediation process on track. As a mediator, dealing with these challenges requires patience, flexibility, empathy, and the ability to 'think on your feet'. While these may seem overwhelming, it's essential to remember that in every challenge lies an opportunity for growth and learning. With the right approach, even the toughest challenges can be transformed into stepping stones towards effective conflict resolution.

In short, successful mediation lies not in the absence of challenges, but in the proactive and progressive overcoming of them. The art of mediation, after all, is not a static discipline but an evolving journey.

Let's journey together on this path of conflict resolution and uncloak the strength in our vulnerabilities.

Chapter 10. Advanced Mediation Techniques: From Theory to Practice

Advanced mediation techniques represent the apex of our shared journey within this report. In this final installment, we shift from the theoretical constructs and foundational principles to their application in the real world.

10.1. Advanced Mediation Techniques: The Toolbox

Advancing beyond the basics of mediation requires thorough knowledge of core mediation principles and an ability to adapt these concepts to the specific context of the negotiation. The task now is to comprehend the dynamic nature of disputes and to actively tailor your approach to each unique situation with agility and creativity.

A critical piece in this puzzle is utilizing "Reflective Listening". This tool presents the opportunity to mirror the speaker's thoughts and feelings, fostering understanding and empathy. A well-executed reflection can dissuade speakers from focusing on the conflict itself and encourage concentration on resolutions instead. The mediator can say, "What I hear you say is..." or "You feel that..." to create an empathetic dialogue environment.

"Reframing", another powerful instrument in the mediator toolkit, is a way to reshape the language and tone of the conversation. The idea is to restate negative or inflammatory comments into neutral or positively charged ones. This shift can help to change the general atmosphere of the negotiation, reducing tensions and promoting dialogue.

Understanding the concept of "Reality Checking", is another advantageous technique for consequential conversations. It introduces a well-guided step back to assess the viability of the demands, solutions, or compromises brought to the negotiation table. This perspective check may lead disputing parties to modify their proposals or reconsider their stands, which can pave the way for the resolution.

10.2. Case in Point: Putting Techniques into Practice

To crystallize the understanding of these techniques, let's follow a hypothetical dispute situation.

Two colleagues, John and Jane are in conflict over the allocation of resources for their respective projects in a company. The mediator, understanding the intensity of the situation, needs to use advanced strategies.

With 'Reflective Listening', the mediator repeats and confirms his understanding of both parties' viewpoints, "It sounds like, John, you feel your project is suffering due to lack of resources, and Jane, you seem to believe your project might be compromised if you share resources."

When tension escalates during the discussion, the mediator uses the 'Reframing' technique. John angrily accuses, "Jane is selfishly hoarding resources." The mediator takes this moment to neutralize the rhetoric, saying, "John is expressing a concern that there might not be enough resources to achieve both projects' goals."

Finally, the mediator applies the 'Reality Checking' technique. After John demands for Jane's entire resource re-allocation, the mediator might ask, "Let's consider the practicality of this solution. How will this impact both projects?"

Through this example, it becomes evident how these advanced mediation techniques create an environment conducive to resolving disputes.

10.3. Mastering Advanced Mediation Techniques: Inner Growth

Transitioning from theory to practice with advanced mediation techniques is no small feat. It requires patience, practice, and a mastering of one's emotional and intellectual self. Remember, too, that in mediation, success isn't necessarily reaching an agreement, it's making sure everyone's voice is heard, the process is fair, and where possible, relationships are preserved and even strengthened.

The first step serves as a challenge to place yourself squarely in the seat of continual learning and practice. Adaptability is crucial: no two disputes are alike, and nuanced situations may require innovative, out-of-the-box thinking. Like stringing beads on a thread, every interaction, every dialogue, every conflict and every resolution can add to your knowledge and expertise.

The second step calls for a deep dive into self-awareness. Mediators must remain aware of their biases while managing high-stake disputes. This involves understanding every reaction, every emotion, every trigger, and every inclination. It's about realizing yourself as an instrument of resolution, where your words, behavior, and presence— by either escalating or resolving the conflict at hand— unleash profound impacts.

Third and finally, embrace compassion: the cornerstone of conflict resolution. Compassion entails demonstrating understanding, empathy and kindness toward disputing parties. As the mediator, your role isn't just to 'fix' the problem. It's to open avenues of communication, to empower individuals, groups or communities to make informed decisions, and to facilitate lasting peaceful relations.

After all, the ripples of effective mediation often extend beyond the immediate dispute, fostering greater understanding, tolerance, and peace within our schools, offices, homes, and societies.

Consequently, mastering advanced techniques in mediation isn't just about honing a professional skill. It's a personal journey of growth, understanding, and enhanced capacity for empathy, equipping us to better navigate and shape the world in which we live.

Chapter 11. Sustaining Peace: The Aftermath of Mediation

The winding road of mediation has, after meandering through chapters of understanding the roots of conflict, the psychology behind it, and the vast methods to mediate it, led us to the crucial juncture of maintaining the achieved peace. With every dealt dispute and every quelled quarrel, lies the necessity to cultivate resilience, sustain the sowed seeds of amity, and ensure they do not dwindle into shadows of their former selves. It is essential to comprehend that the process of mediation doesn't cease when the heated discussions cool down; a significant phase looms ahead - sustaining peace and avoiding recurrence. This chapter delves into these cardinal areas - observing the aftermath of mediation, fortifying the pacific outcomes, and prevention of relapses.

11.1. Aftermath Observations

Progressive results of mediation are like morning dew - fresh, fragile, and prone to evaporation under the sunlight of intolerance, impatience, and misunderstanding. To crystalize the positive outcomes, it becomes imperative to monitor the aftermath

Post-mediation observation captures the nuances of change that semblance of peace brings. This involves paying attention to the behavioral changes in conflicting parties, how they communicate, the level of cooperation, and willingness to sustain peace. Analyzing these elements provides insight into the effectiveness and authenticity of the solution employed, assisting in refining strategies for future conflicts.

The observation process is also a platform to detect the slightest signs of conflict resurfacing and to nip it in the bud. It involves checking in on the parties involved on a regular basis, scrutinizing their adherence with the agreed resolutions, and supporting them in issues they find challenging. This feedback loop enables learning from every mediation and readying the mediators for various future scenarios.

11.2. Fortifying the Outcomes

Upkeep of peace is just as vital as its inception. It's not enough that the tempest has been tamed; it mustn't be allowed to brew again. The fragile peace established post-mediation needs to be fortified to withstand potential storms of contradiction and conflict.

Implementing the accord reached is one aspect. Efficient actualization of mediation results ensures the conflict parties develop faith in the process. It ripens the belief in them that returning to the negotiation table is a worthy endeavor and that the fruits of peace they've tasted are not fleeting pleasures.

The importance of reinforcing the respect and comprehension fostered during the mediation process can't be overstressed. As mediators, one should encourage open communication, poignant empathy, and continued learning. Encourage parties to continue practicing emotional intelligence in their dealings, to interpret conflict cues rightly, and to sustain the habit of active listening. Regular training sessions, workshops, or guidance sessions can be significant in serving this purpose.

11.3. Preventing Recurrences

The ultimate triumph is the absence of the battlefield. A comprehensive approach towards mediation also encompasses preventive measures against recurrent conflicts. There are several techniques to inhibit the factors that could reignite disputes.

Educating all parties involved about conflict and its roots helps discern the calamity before its advent. A demonstrated understanding of human emotions and the complexities of communication can deter one from unintentionally invoking dispute.

Building strong relationships between the parties through team-building exercises, shared goals, and collaborative activities also keeps unrest at bay. A sense of interconnectedness and vested interests in each other's success is a robust defense against the fury of discord.

In conclusion, the art of mediation is an ongoing process that extends far beyond the resolution stage. Its true success lies in the perseverance and persistence displayed in sustaining the hard-earned peace, in firmly anchoring the outcomes, and in armed readiness against future recurrences. This harmonious balance manifests as lasting peace and forms the culmination of the resilient and enriching journey of mediation.

www.ingramcontent.com/pod-product-compliance
Lightning Source LLC
Chambersburg PA
CBHW070942220526
45469CB00007B/2484